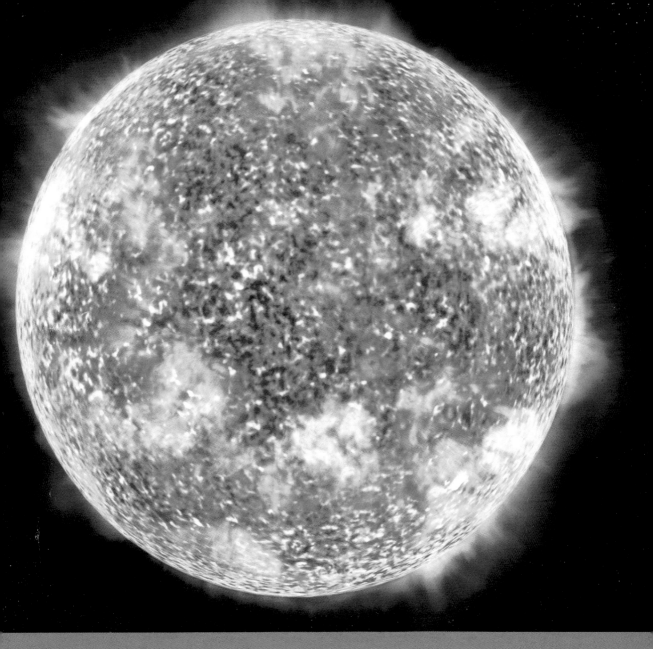

THE SUN

Michael E. Picray

www.av2books.com

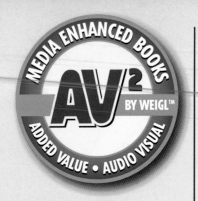

AV² provides enriched content that supplements and complements this book. Weigl's AV² books strive to create inspired learning and engage young minds in a total learning experience.

Your AV² Media Enhanced books come alive with...

 Audio
Listen to sections of the book read aloud.

 Video
Watch informative video clips.

 Embedded Weblinks
Gain additional information for research.

 Try This!
Complete activities and hands-on experiments.

 Key Words
Study vocabulary, and complete a matching word activity.

 Quizzes
Test your knowledge.

 Slide Show
View images and captions, and prepare a presentation.

... and much, much more!

Go to **www.av2books.com**, and enter this book's unique code.

BOOK CODE

U626145

AV² by Weigl brings you media enhanced books that support active learning.

Published by AV² by Weigl
350 5th Avenue, 59th Floor
New York, NY 10118
Website: www.av2books.com   www.weigl.com

Library of Congress Control Number: 2012941989
ISBN 978-1-61913-097-5 (hard cover)
ISBN 978-1-61913-544-4 (soft cover)

Printed in the United States of America in North Mankato, Minnesota
1 2 3 4 5 6 7 8 9   16 15 14 13 12

062012
WEP170512

Editor Aaron Carr
Design Ken Clarke

Every reasonable effort has been made to trace ownership and to obtain permission to reprint copyright material. The publishers would be pleased to have any errors or omissions brought to their attention so that they may be corrected in subsequent printings.

Weigl acknowledges Getty Images as its primary image supplier for this title.

CONTENTS

Most of the energy on Earth comes from the Sun. Even **fossil fuels**, such as coal and oil, come from plants that trapped the Sun's energy millions of years ago. Today, humans can use energy from the Sun directly in the form of solar power. Solar power can be collected as heat, or it can be turned directly into electricity with solar panels. Solar power is a form of energy that has a much lower impact on the environment than fossil fuels.

Studying the Sun

The star that is nearest to Earth shines down on people every day. This star is the Sun. It is the brightest object visible from Earth. The Sun provides Earth with light and heat. There would not be life on Earth without the Sun's energy.

In ancient times, people believed that the Sun was a life-giving force. They knew that this glowing object in the sky gave life to plants, animals, and humans.

■ The Sun is the largest object in the solar system. It is about 864,000 miles (1.4 million kilometers) wide. The Sun could fit the planet Earth across its diameter 109 times.

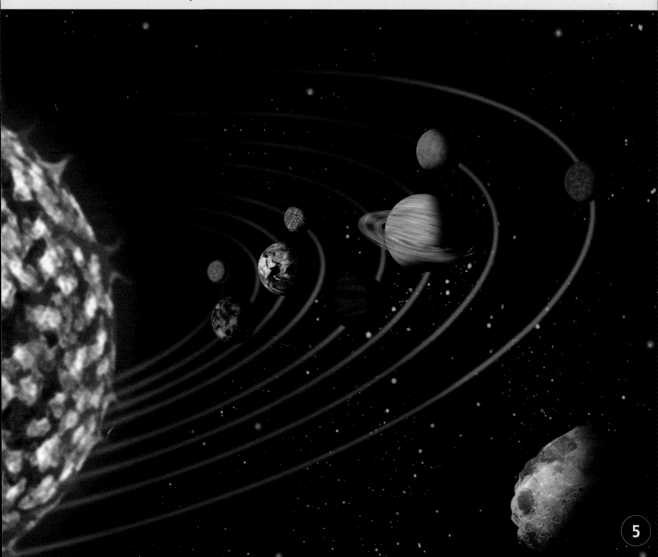

What Is the Sun?

The Sun is a large ball of glowing gas. **Hydrogen** is the main gas that forms the Sun. The temperature of the Sun's surface is about 10,000° Fahrenheit (5,538°Celsius). It is even hotter above and below the surface of the Sun. The Sun's **core** is about 27 million°F (15 million°C).

Stars that formed just after the universe began are called first-generation stars. Second-generation stars formed from the material left behind by first-generation stars. The Sun is a second-generation star.

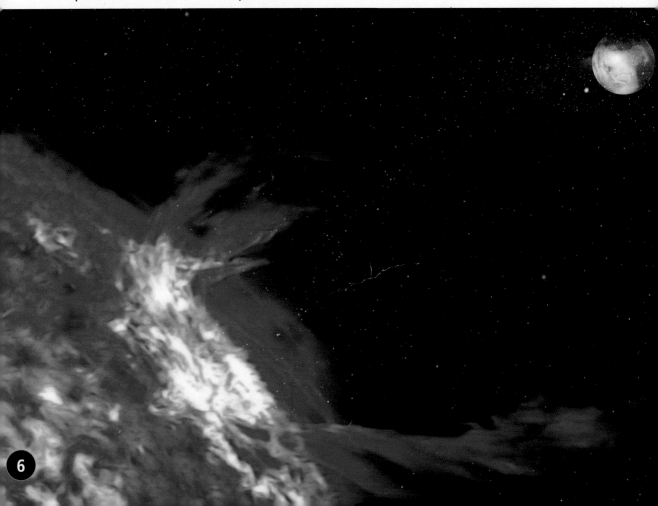

■ The Sun releases energy as a solar wind. This energy travels through the solar system at a speed of 280 miles (450 km) per second.

LAYERS OF THE SUN

1 Corona
The corona is much hotter than any area of the Sun except its core. Some scientists think that the Sun's intense electrical activity may be responsible for this.

2 Chromosphere
This is a thick layer around the outer edge of the Sun. It can only be seen during an eclipse, when the moon blocks most of the Sun's surface from view.

3 Photosphere
The photosphere is the part of the Sun that produces the light people see every day. **Sunspots** also occur on this layer.

4 Convection Zone
This area of the Sun is like a giant storm. Hot pockets of solar gas rise up and fall back toward the core as they cool.

5 Radiative Zone
In this zone, **radiation** from the Sun's core bounces back and forth, losing energy. Eventually, this radiation is released as light.

6 Core
This is the area of the Sun that produces energy. The Sun's strong **gravity** crushes hydrogen together until it becomes helium. This reaction produces the Sun's heat and light.

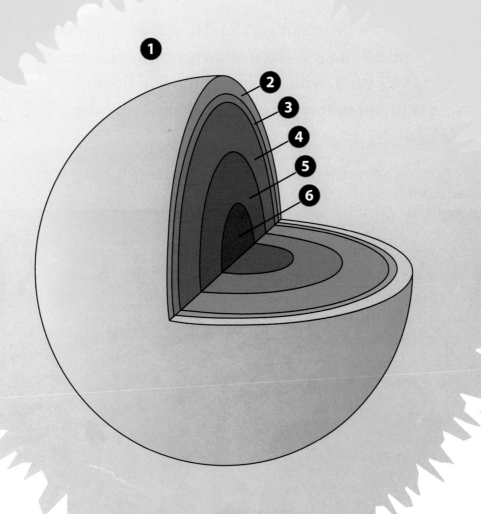

Stories of the Sun

In ancient times, many people admired the Sun because it gave life. People also feared the Sun for its extreme heat. Other ancient peoples prayed to the Sun, believing it to be a powerful god. The ancient Norse and Egyptian people were just two of the many groups who believed that the Sun was a god.

The Norse people called the Sun Sol. They believed that the Sun was a goddess. Sol was chased across the sky every day by a wolf named Skoll.

The Egyptians called their Sun god Ra. He was an important god to the Egyptians. Ra was often shown as having a human body and a hawk's head, with the orb of the Sun floating above it. He was said to travel through the sky every day in a sailing craft.

■ Ancient Egyptians believed Ra called all forms of life into being by calling them by their secret names.

The Fall of Icarus

A Greek **myth** tells about a boy named Icarus. Icarus and his father, Daedalus were in an island prison. To escape, Daedalus made wings of wax and feathers for himself and his son. Icarus and Daedalus used these wings to fly away from the island. Daedalus warned Icarus not to fly too close to the Sun. Icarus did not listen to the warning. The Sun's heat melted the wax, and his wings came apart. Icarus fell to his death.

■ The story of Icarus and Daedalus has been told many times throughout the centuries, in poems, stories, paintings, and sculptures.

Seasons and the Sun

Earth **orbits** the Sun. It takes 365.25 days, or one year, for Earth to complete one orbit. Over the course of this orbit, Earth tilts toward and away from the Sun. The Earth spins like a top while it orbits the Sun. The Sun shines on different parts of the Earth throughout the year. North America tilts towards the Sun in summer. This is why summer is warm. North America tilts away from the Sun in winter. This is why winter is the coldest season.

EARTH'S ROTATION AROUND THE SUN

Earth's tilt is what causes the days to be longer during summer and shorter during winter. For people in the northern half of Earth, or northern hemisphere, the Sun shines at a more direct angle. During winter, the Sun shines at an extreme angle.

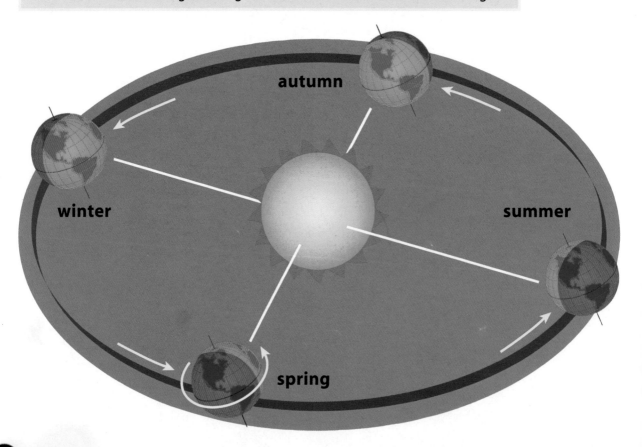

autumn

winter

summer

spring

Solar Energy

The Sun gives off energy in the form of light. This is called solar energy. For thousands of years, people have used the Sun's energy to heat their homes and even to cook. Today, people have invented a new way to use the Sun's energy. Sunlight is turned into electricity using solar panels.

Scientists and engineers have come up with creative ways to use solar power. Deserts get more sunlight than any other place on Earth. Solar panel arrays in deserts across the United States and northern Africa could make as much power as many smaller power plants. Scientists have also thought of using **satellites** to collect solar energy from space. Solar energy may one day become Earth's main energy source.

Scientists estimate that enough solar energy falls on a 100-square-mile (260-square-kilometer) section of the United States to power the whole country.

The Solar System

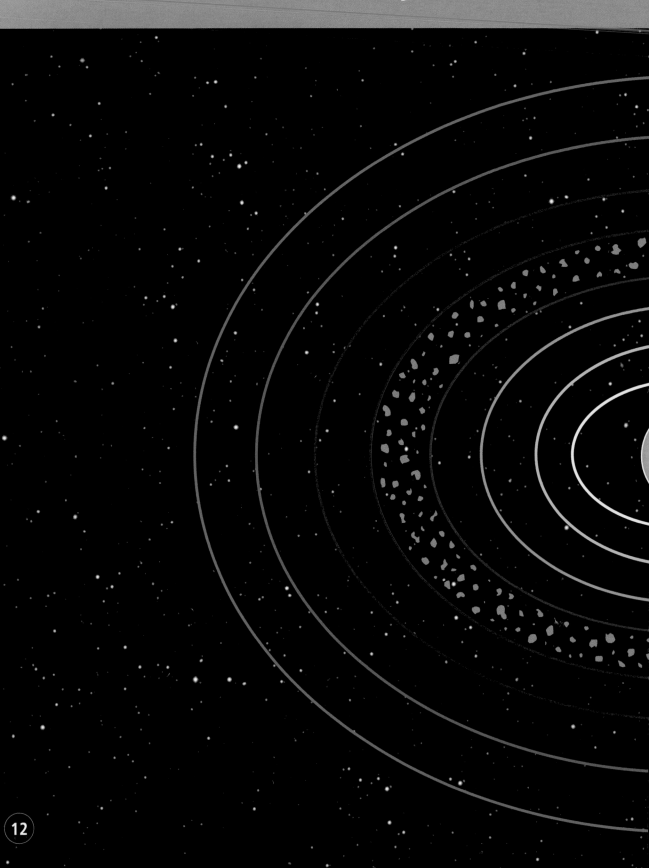

WHAT HAVE YOU LEARNED ABOUT THE SOLAR SYSTEM?

This map shows the planets and other features of the solar system. Use this map, and research in the library and online, to answer these questions.

1. What is the asteroid belt? Where is it located?
2. What is a gas giant? Which planets are gas giants?

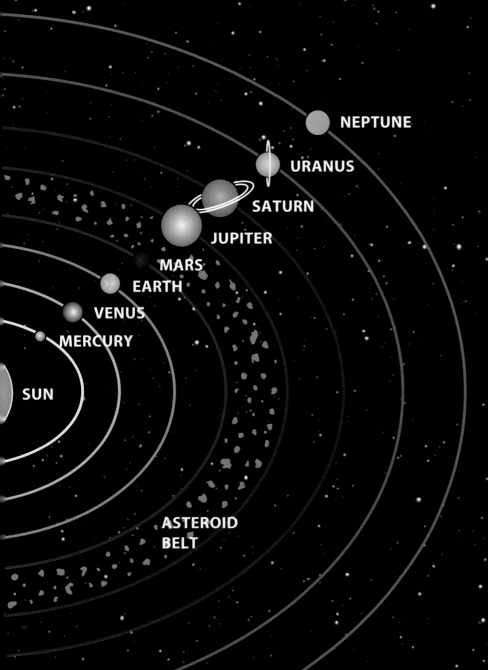

NEPTUNE

URANUS

SATURN

JUPITER

MARS

EARTH

VENUS

MERCURY

SUN

ASTEROID
BELT

The Sun in Nature

All of the world's food requires the Sun's energy to grow. Green plants use the light energy from the Sun to make their food. This process is called photosynthesis. Animals and humans eat plants. They take in the Sun's energy that is stored inside. The Sun's energy also creates weather by heating the air. Wind and storms are caused by warm and cold air moving around each other. Earth would not have wind or rain without the Sun.

A Guiding Light

Humans have used the Sun as a guide for thousands of years. Ancient peoples would use the position of the Sun in the sky to steer their ships. Some animals also use the Sun as a guide.

In the fall, monarch butterflies fly from cool areas to warm areas. They use the Sun as a **compass** when they travel. The location of the Sun in the sky directs their **migration**. Monarch butterflies migrate more than 2,000 miles (3,219 km). These butterflies spend the winter in places such as Mexico and California. In the summer, they can move as far north as Canada and New England.

The monarch butterfly has the longest migration of any animal in North America.

Sun Science

The Sun is an important object of scientific study. Scientists are always trying to learn more about the closest star to Earth. They use satellites, space probes, and **telescopes** to study the Sun. Scientists can also study the Sun from the International Space Station. This space station orbits the Earth.

We know that at least one of the planets orbiting the Sun can support life. By studying the Sun, scientists can look for other planets in the **galaxy** that are similar to Earth. One day in the future, these planets might be places that humans could live.

The Sun produces a kind of light called ultraviolet that can not normally be seen. This light is part of what causes sunburns, and it can be harmful to people and animals. Most of the ultraviolet light produced by the Sun is blocked by a part of Earth's atmosphere called the ozone layer. This layer can be damaged by human-made chemicals. Though many of these chemicals are no longer used, damage has already been done to the ozone layer. Sun safety is always important.

Planet Distances

Eight planets orbit the Sun in our solar system.
Some are close to the Sun, and others are far away.

PLANETS	AVERAGE DISTANCE FROM THE SUN
MERCURY	36 million miles (58 million km)
VENUS	67 million miles (108 million km)
EARTH	93 million miles (150 million km)
MARS	142 million miles (228 million km)
JUPITER	484 million miles (778 million km)
SATURN	886 million miles (1,427 million km)
URANUS	1,784 million miles (2,871 million km)
NEPTUNE	2,795 million miles (4,498 million km)

Sun Safety

Some people think that having a suntan looks healthy. A suntan is actually damaged skin. Damage to the skin is caused by too much sunlight. Sun damage can lead to skin cancer. It also causes wrinkles. This can make people appear older than they really are. Wearing sunscreen protects the skin from the Sun's rays. Clothing can also protect skin from the sun. Anyone who will be outside for long periods of time, either working or playing, should protect themselves from the Sun's rays.

■ A sunscreen's strength is measured by its sun proof factor (SPF). The higher the SPF, the more protection the sunscreen offers from the Sun's rays.

What is an Astronomer?

An astronomer is a scientist who studies objects in space. This includes stars, galaxies, planets, and giant clouds of gas called nebulae.

Astronomers use many tools to study outer space. Telescopes are one important tool. A telescope can record and show light from objects in space, even in types of light that humans cannot normally see. Some telescopes are based on Earth, usually in areas where the air is dry and clear. Other telescopes orbit the Earth in space. This allows the telescopes to take clearer pictures of the stars. Astronomers also use tools such as radio receivers to measure other types of energy in space.

Neil deGrasse Tyson

Neil Tyson was born in Manhattan, New York, in 1958. Since visiting the Hayden Planetarium in Boston at age 9, he had a strong interest in astronomy. Studying at the universities of Harvard, Texas, and Columbia, he earned a doctorate degree in Astrophysics. Today, he is the director of the Hayden Planetarium and a popular voice promoting science. Tyson has hosted television shows, and he was appointed to assist NASA by President George W. Bush.

EQUIPMENT
Some telescopes are so large that they look like buildings. Some of these are on top of Mauna Kea, the highest mountain in Hawai'i. These telescopes measure light and radio waves.

COMPUTERS
Astronomers collect so much data that no human could ever sort through it all. Instead, astronomers run programs on powerful computers. These programs display the data in ways that are helpful to scientists.

Eight Facts About the Sun

The Sun is more than 4.5 billion years old.

The Sun is a type of star called a **yellow dwarf**.

The Sun's gravity is 28 times stronger than Earth's.

Eight planets, including Earth, orbit the Sun.

Earth could fit inside the Sun about 1 million times.

The Sun makes up 99.8 percent of the solar system's mass.

Light from the Sun takes 8 minutes and 32 seconds to reach Earth.

Light from the Sun is sometimes blocked by the Moon. This is called a solar eclipse.

Sun Brain Teasers

1 How long does it take Earth to complete one orbit around the Sun?

2 What is the name of the star closest to Earth?

3 What did the Egyptians call the Sun god?

4 If you could travel to the Sun, would you be able to walk on its surface?

5 What causes Earth's weather?

6 What kind of star is the Sun?

7 How do monarch butterflies migrate to warm areas?

8 Is sunlight good for your skin?

9 What invention allows humans to use the Sun's energy?

10 Would you like to visit the International Space Station?

ANSWERS: 1. 365.25 days, or one year. **2.** The Sun. **3.** Ra. **4.** No. The Sun is too hot to walk on. **5.** The Sun warms the air. **6.** A yellow dwarf star. **7.** Monarch butterflies are guided by the Sun's location in the sky. **8.** Too much Sun damages skin. **9.** Solar panels. **10.** The answer may be yes or no. Give a reason to support your answer.

Cooking with the Sun

The Sun's energy can be very powerful when it is concentrated on a small point. Try the following experiment on a sunny day. This activity should be done with an adult.

Materials Needed

egg

magnifying glass

pan or plate

Directions

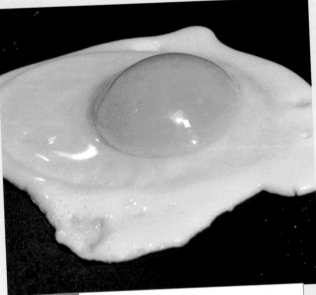

1 Crack open the egg. Gently drip it into the pan or onto the plate.

2 Place the pan or plate containing the egg in direct, bright sunlight.

3 Move your magnifying glass between the Sun and the plate until the Sun shines through the lens in one small, bright point. Depending on the size of the lens, this may be between 3 and 12 inches.

4 Watch the clear egg begin to turn white. This is the energy of the sun beginning to cook the egg.

Key Words

compass: an instrument that shows directions

core: center of something

fossil fuels: fuels that comes from the bodies of dead plants and animals, such as coal and oil

galaxy: a large group of stars

gravity: force that pulls things toward the center

hydrogen: a light, clear gas that burns easily

migration: travels from one place to another

myth: a story or legend, often about gods or heroes

orbit: the circular path a planet makes around an object in the sky, such as the Sun

satellites: orbiting spacecraft

sunspots: temporary dark spots on the surface of the Sun

telescopes: instruments that make distant objects appear closer

yellow dwarf: a star that gives off a yellow glow

Index

Log on to www.av2books.com

AV² by Weigl brings you media enhanced books that support active learning. Go to www.av2books.com, and enter the special code found on page 2 of this book. You will gain access to enriched and enhanced content that supplements and complements this book. Content includes video, audio, weblinks, quizzes, a slide show, and activities.

Audio
Listen to sections of the book read aloud.

Video
Watch informative video clips.

Embedded Weblinks
Gain additional information for research.

Try This!
Complete activities and hands-on experiments.

WHAT'S ONLINE?

Try This!	Embedded Weblinks	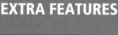 Video	EXTRA FEATURES
Complete a solar power activity.	Learn more about the Sun.	Watch a video about the Sun.	**Audio** Listen to sections of the book read aloud.
Identify the layers of the Sun.	Find out more about the Sun and the solar system.	Watch a video about the solar system.	
Try a solar system mapping activity.	Read more about solar power.		**Key Words** Study vocabulary, and complete a matching word activity.
Test your knowledge of the Sun.	Learn more about how the Sun affects the seasons on Earth.		**Slide Show** View images and captions, and prepare a presentation
			Quizzes Test your knowledge.

AV² was built to bridge the gap between print and digital. We encourage you to tell us what you like and what you want to see in the future.

Sign up to be an AV² Ambassador at www.av2books.com/ambassador.